What If We Do
NOTHING?

POLLUTION

Christiane Dorion

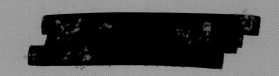

Gareth Stevens
Publishing

Please visit our web site at: www.garethstevens.com.
For a free color catalog describing Gareth Stevens Publishing's list of high-quality books, call 1-800-542-2595 (USA) or 1-800-387-3178 (Canada). Gareth Stevens Publishing's fax: 1-877-542-2596.

Library of Congress Cataloging-in-Publication Data

Dorion, Christiane.
  Pollution / by Christiane Dorion.
    p. cm. – (What if we do nothing?)
  Includes bibliographical references and index.
  ISBN-10: 1-4339-1984-2   ISBN-13: 978-1-4339-1984-8 (lib. bdg.)
  1. Pollution–Juvenile literature.
  2. Environmental protection–Juvenile literature. 3. Sustainable living–Juvenile literature. I. Title.
TD176.D67   2010
363.73–dc22   2008052494

This North American edition published in 2010 by Gareth Stevens Publishing under license from Arcturus Publishing Limited.
Gareth Stevens Publishing
A Weekly Reader® Company
1 Reader's Digest Road
Pleasantville, NY 10570-7000 USA

Copyright © 2009 Arcturus Publishing Limited
Produced by Arcturus Publishing Limited,
26/27 Bickels Yard, 151-153 Bermondsey Street, London SE1 3HA

Series Concept: Alex Woolf
Editor: Alex Woolf
Designer: Phipps Design
Picture Researcher: Alex Woolf

Gareth Stevens Executive Managing Editor: Lisa M. Herrington
Gareth Stevens Editor: Jayne Keedle
Gareth Stevens Senior Designer: Keith Plechaty

Picture Credits:
Arcturus Publishing: 7 (Adam Hook); Corbis: Cover, bottom left (Bettmann), 4 (Liu Liqun), 6 (Roger Wood), 8 (Hulton-Deutsch Collection), 12 (Fritz Hoffmann), 16 (Hans Strand), 23 (Peter Turnley), 24 (Chinch Gryniewicz), 26 (Reuters), 32 (Benjamin Lowy), 34 (Mast Irham/epa), 38 (Gideon Mendel), 39 (Roger Ressmeyer), 42 (Kristy-Anne Glubish/Design Pics); Getty Images: 18 (AFP), 43 (China Photos/Stringer), 44 (Charley Gallay/Stringer); Rex Features: 37 (Paul Cooper); Science Photo Library: Cover, background (Robert Brook), 14 (P. Baeza, Publiphoto Diffusion), 20 (Gary Hincks), cover, top right and 29 (Garry D. McMichael), 31 (Jerry Mason); Shutterstock: 10 (David Máka), 30 (Noam Armonn), 40 (Karen Roach), 41 (Peter Nad); the illustrations on pages 13, 15, and 25 are by Phipps Design.

Cover pictures: Bottom left: Workers on an oil rig spray chemical dispersant on an oil spill in the Bay of Campeche, Gulf of Mexico. Top right: A crop duster sprays insecticide on carrots near McAllen, Rio Grande Valley, Texas. Background: Chemicals from buried industrial waste collect on the ground surface at Heath End, West Midlands, United Kingdom.

Every attempt has been made to clear copyright. Should there be any inadvertent omission, please apply to the publisher for rectification.

Printed in the United States

1 2 3 4 5 6 7 8 9 15 14 13 12 11 10 09

Contents

CHAPTER 1

The State of Our Planet

It is 2025. Wearing a mask to go for a walk or play football is now normal in large cities. Water is very expensive and wars over water sources afflict many countries. More than half of the world's population lives in cities. It is hard to find suitable land for new houses because so much has been contaminated by industry. Air pollution is changing the world's climate. Earth's average temperature is rising, the polar ice caps have nearly melted, and floods affect many cities. How could people believe for so many years that pollution was an acceptable part of progress?

Unintended Consequences

Pollution is the release of harmful substances into the environment by human activity. When we make and use things, we often unintentionally ignore what we create in the process. For example, to make computers, we dig out mountains to extract metals, using and creating toxic substances in the process. We also use energy to transport those metals around the world and release unwanted gases into the air. More energy is used in factories to make the computers, and more chemicals are pumped into the air and poured into rivers. We also use thousands of artificial substances that cannot break down naturally. Instead, they buildup in the environment.

Burning coal to produce electricity is a major cause of air and water pollution. This is a coal power plant in China, the largest coal producer in the world.

When outdated computers are dumped, toxic substances such as lead and mercury can slowly soak into the soil and find their way into the water we drink. Why do we make things this way? Because, for a long time, we thought that the planet was big enough to diffuse those substances over time. We have now reached a level of pollution that Earth can no longer absorb.

THE FIVE DIRTIEST PLACES IN THE WORLD

The following list was produced by looking at the number of people affected, the types of pollutants, and their impact on peoples' health.

City	Country	Sources	Number of People Affected
Sumgait	Azerbaijan	Industrial chemicals oil, heavy metals, and pesticides	275,000
Linfen	China	Cars and coal industry	3,000,000
Tianying	China	Mining and processing of lead and other heavy metals	140,000
Sukinda	India	Mining of chromium	2,600,000
Vapi	India	Production of industrial chemicals and heavy metals	71,000

Source: Blacksmith Institute, 2007

Amazing Earth

Earth is the only planet in the solar system with air to breathe, water to drink, and temperatures that can sustain life. Those amazing conditions are regulated by complex natural systems. Water continuously moves around between land, ocean, and sky. The atmosphere contains the right balance of gases to support life and to protect living things from the Sun's radiation.

Everything in nature is interconnected. Plants have the ability to use the Sun's energy to produce food. When plants and animals die, they decompose and enrich the soil. Human activities are affecting those natural systems. By putting pressure on the environment in one place, it can affect other, often distant places in unpredictable ways.

For example, dangerous chemicals such as mercury and lead have been found in the bodies of people living in the Arctic, thousands of miles from any factory. The wind and ocean currents can carry industrial pollutants far from their original sources.

An Age-Old Problem

Pollution is not new. What is new is the amount and type of pollution we produce and the impact it has on the entire planet. Our early ancestors were nomadic, hunting and moving around in search of food. They produced very little waste — mainly ash from fires and objects made out of stone, wood, and bones.

The Romans were famous for their technology. These public toilets in the Roman town of Dougga, now present-day Tunisia, date from between 100 and 200 B.C. They could seat 12 people. The waste was fed through a drainage system to the town's main drain.

Their waste was biodegradable. That means that it could be broken down naturally by bacteria in the soil. In about 5,000 B.C., people discovered how to smelt copper in open fires to make tools and ornaments. Later, bronze and iron were produced to make better tools, weapons, and armor. The world population was very small and those activities left a tiny amount of waste with little impact on the environment.

Ancient World

Pockets of pollution began to appear as communities grew larger and villages developed into towns and cities. The major civilizations of the ancient world emerged in Mesopotamia, Egypt, India, China, Persia, Greece, and Rome. Those cultures forged metal on a large scale and produced goods by using water power. They burned wood and peat as fuel for cooking and heating.

The Romans made important advancements in engineering. They built sewers to remove human waste and set up a system of garbage collection. They built aqueducts to supply water to cities, and pipes to bring fresh water into their homes. Although Roman cities were fairly clean, the mining and smelting of metals caused pollution. Scientists have even found traces of lead pollution in the ice of Greenland, which came all the way from Roman smelters. Yet most of this early pollution was local and limited in its effects on the environment.

Middle Ages

In medieval Europe, urban pollution increased. Towns and cities were overcrowded, noisy, and dirty. Garbage and waste from butchers, dyers, and other trades were often thrown straight into the street, along with human waste. People were not yet aware of the link between dirty water and the spread of disease.

Wood was the major source of fuel during ancient and medieval times. Due to the needs of an expanding population, the forests began to recede in Europe, and coal became increasingly important for cooking, heating, and powering machinery. By 1400, many European cities were polluted by coal smoke.

In medieval towns, people tipped the contents of their chamber pots out of the windows and into the streets, which had open drains. The usual warning cry was "Gardez l'eau", French for "Beware of the water".

In 1661, the British scientists John Evelyn and John Graunt argued that air pollution could affect plants, wildlife, and people. They suggested moving factories to the countryside and using taller chimneys to reduce the effects of air and water pollution. But many tradesmen were reluctant to give up their prime spots by rivers and near major market places.

Industrial Revolution

Pollution increased dramatically when the Industrial Revolution began in Britain in the late 1700s, spreading to mainland Europe and North America in the 1800s. The invention of power-driven machinery prompted the move away from small workshops producing handmade goods to large-scale factory production. Industrial cities became polluted with fumes from factory chimneys. The factories needed energy to drive

PRODUCTION OF COAL IN BRITAIN, 1700–1900	
1700	2.97 million tons
1750	5.2 million tons
1800	11 million tons
1850	55 million tons
1900	276 million tons

Source: www.historylearningsite.co.uk/coal_mines_industrial_revolution.htm?&0=

Cities like London developed rapidly in the 1800s. This 1872 engraving by Gustave Doré shows the poor, overcrowded living conditions in London's East End.

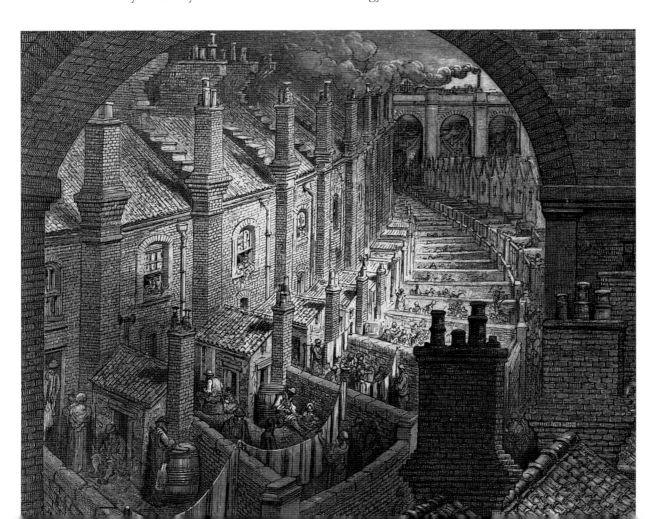

the machines. That energy was provided by burning coal. Coal was also used to heat the homes of city-dwellers. That greatly added to air pollution. Smog (a mixture of smoke and fog) was common in large cities such as Paris and London. In winter, cool air would rise from the river and mix with coal smoke from millions of chimneys to form a thick black fog.

Untreated sewage and industrial waste were often dumped into rivers. By the 1850s, water pollution in major cities had become a serious problem. The River Thames, the main source of drinking water for London, became a cesspool of human waste from nearly 3 million people. Diseases carried by rats and fleas became common. Epidemics of cholera and typhoid fever decimated small populations in towns and villages across Europe. Scientists began to understand the link between water pollution and outbreaks of disease. To combat the spread of disease, sewers were built in European and North American cities to divert human waste to rivers and seas.

SERIOUS EPISODES OF SMOG, 1892–1952

When?	Where?	Why?	Impact
1892	London, U.K.	Burning of coal and fog	Deaths of 1,000 people
1948	Donora, Pennsylvania	Toxic gases from zinc smelting plant and fog	Deaths of 70 people and thousands hospitalized
1952	London, U.K.	Burning of coal and fog	Deaths of 4,000 people

Source: www.enviropedia.org.uk/Air_Quality/Smog/php

Modern World

During the 1900s, the world's population rose dramatically. Manufacturers developed new products to appeal to a growing class of wealthy consumers. Cars, radios, televisions, and home appliances were among the most popular products of the century. Manufacturers produced newer, slightly different products each year. By using clever marketing techniques, they persuaded customers that the goods they had bought the previous year were now out of date. That attitude helped increase pollution levels as perfectly good products were discarded in favor of the latest models.

Since the 1940s, a wider range of products has been developed that include parts made up of plastics, synthetic fabrics and dyes, antibiotics, and pesticides, which improved the lives of millions of people. However, many of those substances do not decompose naturally and instead buildup in the environment.

Nuclear power, also developed in the 1940s, promised a new, less expensive source of energy. But nuclear power produces radioactive waste, which remains dangerous for thousands of years.

In the late 1900s, other countries, such as China, India, and Brazil, also launched massive industrialization programs. That led to a major increase in pollution from cars, factories, mines, and farms. The lower labor costs of those newly industrialized nations meant that goods could be sold even more cheaply, fueling a boom in retail sales around the world. As prices fell for products, such as clothing and electronic goods, people consumed more, threw away more, and further added to pollution.

Since the 1980s, the high-tech boom has produced a new type of pollution from discarded electronic and electrical equipment such as computers, televisions, game consoles, and mobile phones. Those machines can release toxic chemicals into the environment, such as lead, mercury, and cadmium.

A Different Way of Thinking

Modern life creates pollution. We make, use, and dispose of things, often without giving much thought to the effect it has on the environment. We start by extracting resources. We then produce objects, distribute them, and consume them. Finally, we dump what is not needed anymore. That doesn't happen in nature. Earth's natural systems, like the water cycle, recycle and reuse all materials. In nature, there is no such thing as waste or pollution. Waste from one animal is food for another.

Developments in science and technology have led to enormous improvements in our lives. However, each new development has come at a price. We buy products only to discard them soon after, responding to the latest fashion or trend. It is often cheaper to buy a new television than to have an older model repaired. Many products we buy, such as plastic cups, cameras, and batteries, are designed to be used only briefly before being thrown away. They are made of artificial materials that do not decompose easily or quickly. Instead, they buildup in the environment and affect the quality of the air we breathe, the water we drink, and the soil in which we grow our food.

WHAT WOULD YOU DO?

You Are in Charge

You are representing your school in a regional youth forum to discuss the problem of pollution in your area. Which proposals, do you think, will best address that problem?

- Find out what the main sources of pollution are in your area and stage protests against the polluters.
- Force the factories or people responsible for polluting the environment to pay for the clean up by imposing fines.
- Push the government to set stricter standards for pollution.
- Provide information on air, water, and ground pollution levels in your area and send letters to local residents informing them of problems.

CHAPTER 2

The Air We Breathe

It is 2025. Maria's family lives in an apartment in Los Angeles. Today, the weather forecast predicts another "code red" day. People are advised to stay indoors because the air quality is poor. As a safety measure, Maria's school is closed. It used to be rare to miss school, but that is happening more often as the climate is changing. Few people go outside on hot days when brown smoke hangs over the city. That air is heavy with fumes from factories, waste incinerators, cars, and trucks. Next year, Maria is going to a "virtual" school so she can learn from home through Internet-based tutoring.

Our Unique Atmosphere

The atmosphere is a thin blanket of gases that surrounds Earth. It is essential for the survival of life on the planet. The atmosphere moves heat and water around the globe and protects living things from the Sun's harmful radiation. Our atmosphere has just the right balance of chemicals to sustain life. Those move around continuously between sky, ocean, soil, plants, and animals. For example, trees absorb carbon dioxide from the air and produce oxygen. When trees die, carbon is released back into the atmosphere.

A very thin layer around Earth, called the troposphere, is the only part of the atmosphere in which living things can breathe. About 78 percent of the air we breathe is made of nitrogen, and 21 percent is oxygen. The rest is made of other gases such as water vapor and carbon dioxide.

Like many industrial cities, Kaohsiung, Taiwan, suffers from air pollution. People often wear face masks to protect themselves from the fumes.

Before the expansion of cities and the development of industry, Earth's natural systems kept the air clean. Wind dispersed fumes and rain washed dust into the ground, rivers, and seas. Since the Industrial Revolution, humans have disrupted the delicate balance of the atmosphere by releasing more pollutants in the air than nature can diffuse. Air pollution has become a global problem.

What Is Air Pollution?

Air pollution is gases, dust, and fumes in the air that can harm people, animals, and plants. Those gases, dust, and fumes are called pollutants. Some pollutants are visible, like smoke from car exhausts, and dust. Others are invisible, like emissions from cattle or chemicals released by factories. Some pollutants are the result of natural disasters, such as forest fires and erupting volcanoes. However, most air pollution comes from a single human activity: the burning of fossil fuels. We burn fossil fuels, such as oil and coal, to power cars and factories and to produce electricity.

MAIN SOURCES OF AIR POLLUTION

Substance	Combustion of fuel in cars and other vehicles	Burning of fossil fuels to power factories	Burning of fossil fuels to produce energy in power stations	Disposal of waste in landfill sites	Burning of waste in incinerators	Emissions from intensive cattle farming
Carbon dioxide	✖	✖	✖			
Carbon monoxide	✖	✖	✖		✖	
Sulfur dioxide		✖	✖			
Nitrogen oxides	✖	✖	✖			
Particulates	✖	✖	✖		✖	
Methane		✖	✖	✖		✖
Heavy metals (e.g. lead, mercury, and cadmium)	✖	✖	✖	✖	✖	

Source: Data compiled from U.K. Air Quality Archive; U.K. Department for Environment, Food and Rural Affairs; Environment Agency

Transportation

Cars are a major source of air pollution. Car engines burn a mixture of air and gasoline vapor. That releases tiny particles of chemicals and gases into the atmosphere made up of carbon monoxide, carbon dioxide, and nitrogen oxides. Breathing those toxic gases and tiny particles can cause lung cancer and heart disease.

Some of those gases react with other gases once they are released into the air. Those changed gases are called secondary pollutants. For example, waste gases from cars react with sunlight to form a gas called ozone, which is a form of oxygen. The effect is smog. That is different from the smog in cities hundreds of years ago. It is photochemical smog — a brownish haze that floats over cities, most often on warm, sunny days. Los Angeles and Mexico City are badly affected by smog.

Other Sources of Air Pollution

Power stations are another major source of air pollution. When we burn fossil fuels to generate power for homes, offices, and factories, we release carbon dioxide and other harmful gases into the air.

Factories also contribute to air pollution. Each industry produces a different type. Metal production is the main industrial source of air pollution, releasing sulfur dioxide and highly toxic heavy metals into the air. Exposure to those chemicals can affect people's health in many ways. Steel factories, paper mills, and chemical and cement plants all produce massive quantities of fine, toxic particles.

Intensive farming is another cause of air pollution. Spraying fertilizers to enrich the soil and pesticides to kill insects releases harmful chemicals such as nitrous oxide into the air. Large amounts of manure from cattle farming produce toxic gases such as ammonia. The digestive gases emitted by cattle pollute the air with methane.

> ### CAR FACTS
>
> There are 622 million cars around the world today.
> In 2007, about 52 million cars were produced in factories.
> In one year, the average car can produce three to four times its own weight in carbon dioxide.

Source: World Resources Institute

Santiago, Chile's capital city, is badly affected by smog. The city lies in a valley, bordered by the Andes Mountains. The mountains trap pollutants from cars and factories over the city for days at a time.

Methane traps heat in the atmosphere and contributes to global warming (see pages 16–17).

The way we dispose of our waste also causes air pollution. Burning waste releases dangerous chemicals such as dioxins and heavy metals into the air. It also produces toxic ashes. Burying waste in landfills produces harmful substances, such as methane and lead.

The Carbon Cycle

How does burning fossil fuels produce pollution? Examining the carbon cycle helps us understand. All living things contain carbon. Carbon is also in the oceans, air, and rocks. In the atmosphere, carbon is attached to oxygen in a gas called carbon dioxide. Plants absorb carbon dioxide and sunlight to make their own food, and they release oxygen. That process is called photosynthesis. The carbon becomes part of the plant. Animals take in carbon when they eat plants and other animals.

This diagram shows the natural processes that move carbon around Earth. Carbon atoms are constantly being exchanged between one living thing and another, and between living things and the environment. However, the total amount of carbon on Earth always remains the same.

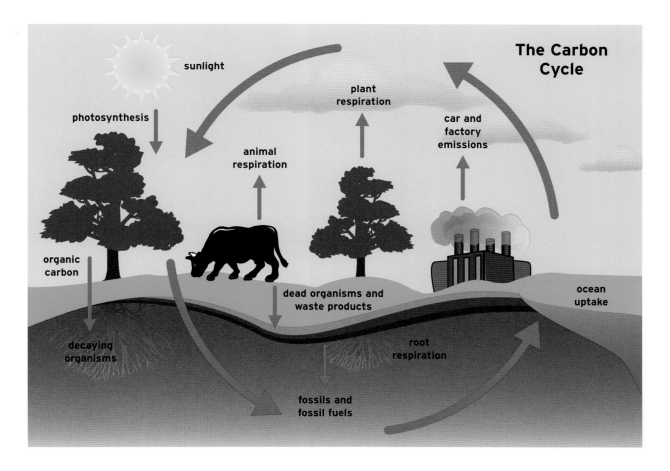

The Carbon Cycle

sunlight

plant respiration

photosynthesis

car and factory emissions

animal respiration

organic carbon

dead organisms and waste products

ocean uptake

decaying organisms

root respiration

fossils and fossil fuels

Carbon is released back into the atmosphere (as carbon dioxide) when animals exhale and when their remains decompose in the soil. Fossil fuels such as coal, oil, and natural gas also come from the remains of plants and tiny marine animals. Those remains are buried in the soil and compressed by heat and pressure over time. Fossil fuels take millions of years to form. When we burn fossil fuels to produce energy, that carbon is unlocked and released back into the air as carbon dioxide.

Today we release much more carbon dioxide into the air than Earth's plants and oceans can absorb. We are also cutting down large areas of forest, so there are fewer trees to absorb existing carbon.

Global Warming

Most scientists believe that the burning of fossil fuels is affecting Earth's climate. Earth is getting warmer. That increase in temperature is causing the oceans to expand, polar ice caps to melt, and sea levels to rise.

Polar bears could be extinct within 20 years because of global warming. As the Arctic sea ice melts, they are forced to swim farther in their hunt for food.

To understand how global warming is happening, it helps to think of the atmosphere as a kind of greenhouse. When sunlight heats Earth's surface, some of that heat is reflected back into space. However, much of the heat gets trapped in the atmosphere by natural gases, such as water vapor, carbon dioxide, and methane. They are like the glass walls of a greenhouse, keeping Earth warm. Without those natural greenhouse gases, heat would escape back into space and Earth would be too cold to sustain life.

The problem is that since we began burning fossil fuels on a large scale during the Industrial Revolution, too much heat from the Sun is getting trapped in the atmosphere. As a result, Earth is growing warmer.

Burning fossil fuels releases carbon dioxide, which accounts for 80 percent of human-made greenhouse gases. Another important greenhouse gas is methane. It is produced from the decay of garbage in landfills and the extraction of coal and natural gas. Scientists estimate that the digestive gases emitted by cattle produce between 15 and 20 percent of global methane emissions.

Acid Rain

When we burn fossil fuels in power stations, factories, houses, and cars, we produce toxic gases such as sulfur dioxide and nitrogen oxides. Those react with other gases in the atmosphere to form strong acids. They mix with tiny droplets of water in the air and then fall back to the ground as acid rain, snow, or hail. Strong winds can carry those chemicals over long distances. The acid rain in Scandinavia, for instance, is caused by emissions from the United Kingdom and other northern European countries. Acid rain damages trees and plants and makes lakes and rivers more acidic, harming fish and other wildlife.

This chart shows the proportion of global greenhouse gas emissions created by different types of human activity.

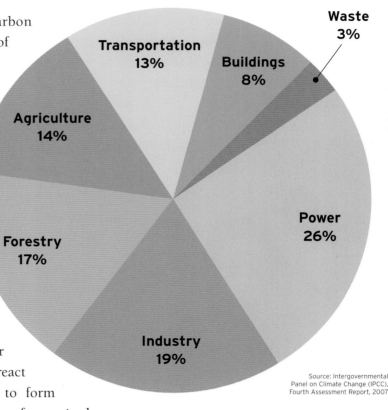

Waste 3%
Transportation 13%
Buildings 8%
Agriculture 14%
Power 26%
Forestry 17%
Industry 19%

Source: Intergovernmental Panel on Climate Change (IPCC), Fourth Assessment Report, 2007

Holes in the Ozone Layer

About 9 to 19 miles (14 to 31 kilometers) above Earth is a layer of atmosphere that contains high concentrations of a gas called ozone. Life on Earth could not survive without the protective shield of the ozone layer. That ozone layer protects life on Earth by absorbing the Sun's harmful ultraviolet rays, preventing most of them from reaching Earth's surface. Those rays cause skin to tan, but too much exposure to them can cause skin cancer.

Each spring, a hole as big as North America forms in the ozone layer over the South Pole. A smaller hole develops over the North Pole. Those depleted ozone holes have been caused by a group of polluting gases known as chlorofluorocarbons (CFCs). CFCs were first produced in the 1930s. They were used in spray cans, refrigerators, air conditioning systems, and fire extinguishers.

Scientists discovered that, high in the atmosphere, chlorine atoms escape from CFCs, destroying the ozone layer. In 1996, most industrialized countries banned CFCs, but those gases will remain in

This photo shows victims of one of the world's worst industrial disasters, in Bhopal, India. In 1984, toxic gas leaked from the Union Carbide pesticide factory and floated over the crowded city. Thousands of people died instantly and many more were injured.

the atmosphere for a long time. They are also released when old refrigerators and air conditioning units are dumped in landfills.

Dangerous Leaks

Accidents in chemical factories and nuclear power plants can cause large-scale environmental distruction. One of the biggest disasters of this kind occurred in Bhopal, India, in 1984. A Union Carbide pesticide factory leaked toxic gases that drifted over the city. Between 15,000 and 20,000 people died and as many as 200,000 were injured.

Accidents at nuclear power plants can cause the release of high levels of radiation. People who are exposed to too much radiation can suffer tissue damage and diseases, such as cancer. The world's worst nuclear accident occurred in 1986 at the Chernobyl Nuclear Power Plant in Ukraine. An explosion at the plant sent a radioactive cloud over much of Western Europe. More than 56 people were killed instantly, but the health of thousands more was affected. In the years following the accident, instances of cancer and birth defects rose dramatically in the region.

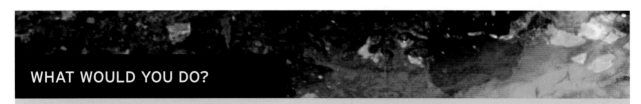

WHAT WOULD YOU DO?

You Are in Charge

You are taking part in a debate on how to combat global warming. Which of the following statements do you support? Why?

- Global warming is not caused by human activity. It is a natural phenomenon, and we should not be concerned about it.
- We can reduce air pollution by developing new technologies to reduce carbon emissions from factories and vehicles.
- We can reduce air pollution by using nuclear power, as it does not involve burning fossil fuels.
- We can reduce air pollution by using renewable sources of energy, such as wind and solar power.
- We can reduce air pollution by reducing our energy use.

CHAPTER 3

Every Drop Counts

It is 2025. An old woman is sitting with her granddaughter by the River Ganges in Calcutta, India. "When I was young," she says, "this was a sacred river where we used to scatter the ashes of our loved ones according to Hindu tradition. The river was pure. At times, you would see garlands of flowers floating on it. The river was alive and fishermen came here to find food. Today, the River Ganges is smelly and lifeless. It has become the city's dump. Every day, raw sewage and factory waste are pumped into the river. That is why we are short of clean water. We are at war with other countries fighting over water sources because we have destroyed our own."

The Water Cycle

The water you drink has been recycled over and over for more than 3.5 billion years! Since the formation of Earth, the same water has been continuously recycled. The Sun's heat causes water in rivers, lakes, and seas to evaporate. The water vapor cools as it rises and turns back into tiny water droplets to form clouds.

This diagram shows how water is continuously on the move around Earth. The amount of water on Earth is constant and it keeps moving as ice, liquid, or gas, between land, ocean, and sky.

When the clouds become too heavy, water falls back to Earth as rain, hail, or snow.

Some water falls directly into lakes and oceans. Some collects into rivers and streams before returning to larger bodies of water, where it evaporates again. Some soaks slowly into the ground to become part of the groundwater, a huge underground reservoir of freshwater for plants and animals. Plants release water back into the atmosphere through a process called transpiration. And the cycle goes on.

As the world population grows and industry expands, the demand for water increases. However, the amount of water on Earth is limited. By pumping polluting gases into the air, spraying chemicals on the soil, and dumping waste into rivers and seas, we are reducing the amount of clean water left on Earth.

What Is Water Pollution?

Water pollution occurs when unwanted substances end up in rivers, lakes, seas, and groundwater. That harms plants, animals, and people. Water can be polluted deliberately by the dumping of harmful substances, such as sewage or factory waste, directly into water sources. To reduce that type of pollution, most industrialized countries have adopted strict laws.

Water can also be polluted unintentionally, by substances produced far away that are transported by rain, rivers, and ocean currents. As rain flows over the ground, it carries toxic substances from farms, industrial sites, mines, building sites, gardens, roads, and garbage dumps. Those substances end up in streams, rivers, lakes, and oceans. They also soak into the soil, affecting the groundwater.

Top: Freshwater makes up a small fraction of Earth's total water supply.

Bottom: This diagram shows the sources of Earth's freshwater. Most freshwater is stored in ice caps and glaciers.

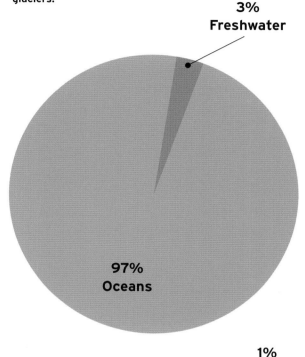

3%
Freshwater

97%
Oceans

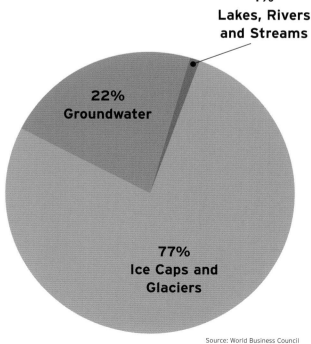

1%
Lakes, Rivers
and Streams

22%
Groundwater

77%
Ice Caps and
Glaciers

Source: World Business Council
for Sustainable Development

Ocean currents move massive amounts of water and pollutants around the globe. In 1992, a cargo ship traveling from Hong Kong to the United States hit a storm in the Pacific Ocean. Many containers were washed overboard, including one with thousands of bath toys. Since then those plastic ducks have been found all over the world from Hawaii to Iceland and the North Pole. Water pollution does not recognize national borders. It is a global problem.

Opposite: Nearly all the major rivers in the world are affected by industrial pollution. The pulp and paper industry is a major source of pollution. Here, waste water from a paper mill is being discharged straight into China's Qingai River.

Pollution From Industry

Nearly all the lakes, rivers, and oceans of the world contain some level of industrial pollution. Factories use large amounts of water to make, wash, and dilute products. After the water is used, it is put back into rivers, along with any toxic waste produced in the process. Governments in many countries have laws to ensure that waste water is cleaned before it is released. Despite that, factories in many parts of the world continue to dump unfiltered industrial waste into rivers and seas. That industrial waste contains toxic substances such as lead, asbestos, and mercury. Many of those substances do not break down naturally over time. Instead, they buildup in the environment and can be harmful to plants and animals.

One such substance is mercury. Mercury can damage the nervous and reproductive systems of mammals, including humans. Mercury is emitted mainly by coal-fired power plants, and also by smelting and cement production. When mercury waste ends up in the sea, it is absorbed by tiny creatures called phytoplankton. When the phytoplankton are eaten by small fish, the mercury stays in those fish. The small fish are in turn eaten by larger fish, such as tuna, which then become food for people and animals. The result is that large amounts of mercury end up in animals at the top of the food chain. That is called bioaccumulation.

THE TIME IT TAKES FOR DIFFERENT ITEMS TO DEGRADE IN WATER

Cardboard	2 weeks
Newspaper	6 weeks
Foam	50 years
Styrofoam	80 years
Aluminum	200 years
Plastic	Between 400 years and forever
Glass	It takes so long to degrade that we don't know the exact time.

Source: www.water-pollution.org.uk/marine.html

Pollution From Sewage

Sewage is a major source of water pollution. It is biodegradable, so small amounts can break down naturally in the soil. However, the human population of 6.7 billion produces a huge amount of sewage, and Earth cannot absorb it naturally. The problem is made worse by the vast quantity of artificial substances we flush down our drains. Those are not biodegradable. Every day we use shampoos, soaps, toothpastes, detergents, hair dyes, and cleaning products. Many of those mixtures contain synthetic, or artificial, chemicals. Have you ever wondered where all those chemicals go?

In industrialized countries, most sewage is carried away from homes through a network of pipes and ends up in treatment plants. There the sewage is cleaned by chemicals and bacteria, which eat germs and dirt. The cleaned water is pumped back into the nearest river. In some countries, the sludge, or solid leftovers, is dumped in landfill sites or burned in incinerators. In others, it is turned into fertilizers to enrich the soil. However, some toxic substances remain in the water, even after treatment.

In many developing countries, many people do not have access to safe drinking water. Most sewage is discharged directly into rivers and streams without any treatment. About 40 percent of the world's population lives in areas without treatment facilities and where there is no collection of sewage. Each year, more than 5 million people die from diseases such as cholera, diarrhea, and typhoid fever. People catch those diseases by drinking water polluted with sewage.

In many developing countries, raw sewage is pumped directly into the sea with little or no treatment. As it contains high levels of nitrogen, ammonia, and other contaminants, it can create serious problems for marine life and swimmers.

Pollution From Agriculture

Since the beginning of the 1900s, farmers have used intensive farming techniques to boost their yields and satisfy the demand of the world's growing population. Today, intensive farming relies on the use of herbicides, pesticides, and fertilizers. Those are sprayed on fields to kill weeds and insects or to boost the growth of food crops. They contain toxic chemicals such as nitrogen and phosphorus. When it rains, those chemicals are washed through the soil and end up in nearby rivers and lakes. Medications and hormones used by farmers to make animals grow larger and more quickly also end up in the water supply.

Chemical fertilizers and manure from farm animals contain nutrients such as nitrates and phosphates. Sometimes those fertilizers run off into nearby rivers and lakes, causing an increase in nutrients. Too many nutrients in the water cause plants and algae to grow very fast. The water becomes cloudy and green. That high density of algae is called an algal bloom. The algae may absorb all the oxygen in the water, leaving little for plants and fish. Algae also blocks sunlight for plants living under the water's surface. About half the lakes in Asia, Europe, and North and South America are polluted by algal blooms.

MAIN SOURCES OF WATER POLLUTION

Pollutant	Industrial waste	Waste from cars carried by wind, rain, and run-off water	Sewage	Agricultural waste	Mining waste	Household waste	Waste from landfills leaching into the ground
Organic Matter (Plant/Animal Waste)	✖		✖	✖			✖
Nutrients	✖		✖	✖			
Heavy Metals	✖	✖			✖		✖
Oil	✖	✖	✖	✖		✖	✖
Toxic Chemicals	✖	✖	✖	✖	✖	✖	✖

Source: www.earthtrends.wri.org

Oil and Water Do Not Mix

Major oil tanker spills often make the headlines as they can have devastating effects on marine environment. One of the worst oil spills occurred in 1989 when the *Exxon Valdez* sank off the coast of Alaska. The tanker ran aground on rocks and spilled 10.5 million gallons (40 million liters) of crude oil into the sea. The oil eventually covered 11,000 square miles (28,000 square kilometers) of ocean, more than 22,000 times the surface of an Olympic swimming pool. Thousands of fish, ducks, sea otters, seals, and seabirds died.

Oil cannot dissolve in water and forms a thick sludge. It suffocates fish, gets caught in the feathers of marine birds, and blocks light for aquatic plants. It also affects people whose livelihood depends on fishing and tourism in coastal areas.

In 2000, the oil tanker *Al Jazya 1* sank off the coast of the United Arab Emirates in bad weather. It spilled 330 tons (300 tonnes) of oil and caused a 2,953 foot-long (900-meter-long) oil slick.

Accidental spills from oil tankers make up only about 12 percent of the oil that enters the oceans. The rest comes from ships flushing their tanks out at sea, and from oil platforms and motorboats. Large volumes of oil are also poured down the drain or carried into the sea by rain. Rainwater picks up drips of oil from cars, gas stations, tractors, leaky storage tanks, and industrial machinery.

Plastic Pollution

Plastic is the most common material manufactured today. It is popular because it is light, durable, and cheap to produce. It can also be easily molded into different shapes. Also, plastic does not break down easily. Its molecules are very large and tightly bonded together and they resist decomposition. For those reasons, plastic makes up a very large proportion of today's pollution. It is estimated that 90 percent of all the garbage floating in the oceans is plastic. If you go to a beach anywhere in the world, you are likely to see plastic trash washed up by the waves.

Plastic pollution can harm seabirds, fish, and other marine animals. According to conservation groups, millions of seabirds and 100,000 mammals and sea turtles die each year by getting entangled in fishing lines and nets or by swallowing tiny pieces of plastic. About 80 percent of plastic pollution comes from items that have been thrown away on land and are then carried out to sea by rivers, wind, and tides. The rest comes from private and commercial ships, oil platforms, and spilled containers from cargo ships.

Scientists have recently discovered a huge area of plastic waste twice the size of Texas, floating in the northern Pacific Ocean. A slow, swirling current traps plastic debris from all over the world. They named it the Great Pacific Garbage Patch and predicted that it will double in the next decade.

WHAT WOULD YOU DO?

You Are in Charge

A 20-year-old tanker carrying tons of crude oil strikes rocks in a storm. The tanker begins to leak oil into the ocean. Who is responsible?

- The oil company that hired the ship to transport oil to the refinery is responsible.

- The ship's captain who was in charge of the vessel is responsible.

- Consumers, who demand oil for their energy needs, are responsible.

- Governments are responsible because they failed to pass laws preventing unsafe vessels from being used.

What can be done to avoid such a disaster in the future?

CHAPTER 4

Soaking Into the Soil

It is 2025. Four years ago, the Jones family bought the house of their dreams. It is in the center of town, so the family can walk or cycle to school, to work, and to the local stores. Yet the house is in a quiet location and has a big yard. Last year, the whole family developed breathing problems, allergies, and skin rashes. Their neighbors also began to suffer similar health problems. The local community discovered that at the beginning of the century, dangerous waste had been buried underground in containers about 12 miles (19 km) away. Scientists reassured the population that those hi-tech containers were safe and could not leak toxic pollution into the soil, but the Joneses and their neighbors do not believe them.

What Is Land Pollution?

Land pollution occurs when unwanted substances end up on the land or in the ground. The main cause of land pollution is the production and disposal of consumer goods and intensive farming. To make things in factories, we extract tons of raw materials, such as metals, sand, and crude oil, leaving heaps of mining waste behind. That waste often contains toxic substances that will contaminate the soil.

As the world population rises, production increases to keep pace with demand. The amount of garbage we throw away increases. We are also creating more synthetic substances that do not decompose naturally. Those substances accumulate in the environment.

The demand for food is also increasing, so we farm the land more intensively, spraying chemicals to boost productivity and to get rid of weeds and insects. Those chemicals slowly soak into the ground.

NEW CHEMICALS FOR INDUSTRY

At least 100,000 synthetic chemicals are used by industry today and more than 700 new ones are added each year. Very few chemicals have been tested for their effects on plants and animals.

Source: www.storyofstuff.com

Flammable, explosive, or poisonous waste is buried in underground containers, which sometimes leak into the soil.

A Chemical World

In 1962, Rachel Carson, an American biologist, wrote a famous book called *Silent Spring*. In it she describes the danger of using strong chemicals such as dichloro-diphenyl-trichloroethane (DDT). That is one of the most powerful pesticides ever produced and can kill hundreds of different kinds of insects at once. Carson explained how chemicals like DDT accumulate in the food chain and end up poisoning birds and animals. Her book launched the global environmental movement and led to a worldwide ban of DDT. However, since then, many other chemicals have been developed. Those are used all over the world to make food, clothes, furniture, electric appliances, and cars. When those products are disposed of, many of the toxic substances used to make them remain in the environment, polluting the soil, air, and water.

A plane sprays pesticide on carrot crops in the Rio Grande Valley in Texas. The use of toxic chemicals for intensive farming is a major source of soil pollution and many people campaign to ban their use.

The Journey of a Cell Phone

Each human-made product creates a huge amount of pollution, both at the start and the end of its life. Have you ever thought about the pollution produced by just one cell phone? The world has more than three billion cell phones. Nearly half of them are made in China, but the raw materials come from all over the world. Each phone contains about 400 different parts. Those include handsets, circuit boards, keypads, and batteries.

A large percentage of the pollution caused by producing cell phones comes from the extraction of raw materials. The circuit board is made from copper, gold, lead, nickel, zinc, beryllium, tantalum, coltan, and other metals. Batteries contain nickel, cobalt, zinc, cadmium, and copper. To extract those substances, raw materials need to be mined around the world and refined in factories. Mining involves clearing forests, digging pits, and using chemicals to extract ore from rock, leaving behind tons of toxic mud. Fossil fuels are also burned to transport those raw materials and to assemble the phones in factories.

There are more than three billion cell phones currently in circulation around the world. Those phones are constantly being discarded, releasing their toxic components into the environment.

Valuable natural resources, such as trees (for paper), crude oil (for plastic), aluminum, and other materials are used to package the phones once they are made. The phones are then transported to their destinations around the world, consuming yet more fossil fuels and producing more pollution in the process.

Yet most cell phones are thrown away after two years and end buried in landfill sites. All the valuable gold, silver, copper, and other resources inside them can never be retrieved. Some of the substances inside cell phones are known as persistent toxins. Those poisons can stay in the environment for long periods of time. They can leach into the ground and find their way into our water.

What about recycling? Old cell phones are often sent to China, Pakistan, and India, where people dismantle them by hand to recover the valuable materials. Even so, the leftovers are often dumped in fields, ponds, and rivers, polluting the land and water of other countries. And this is the story of just one product!

Here are some of the parts of a cell phone. Dismantling old cell phones for recycling is slow and expensive as it has to be done manually. Researchers are examining more efficient ways of recovering valuable materials and disposing toxic phone parts.

COMPUTERS

More than a billion computers are now in use worldwide. In 2007, about 268 million computers were sold. Sixty-seven million of them were bought in the United States alone. It is predicted that 426 million computers will be sold worldwide in 2012. The manufacture of a new computer and monitor uses 8.5 ounces (241 grams) of fossil fuels, 49 pounds (22 kg) of chemicals, and 396 gallons (1,500 liters) of water. A PC is typically 40 percent steel, 30–40 percent plastic, 10 percent aluminum, and 10 percent other metals, including copper, gold, silver, cadmium, and platinum.

Source: www.e-takeback.org

Landfills and Incinerators

What happens to all the industrial and domestic waste we produce? In many countries, the garbage is collected and taken to landfills, where it is carefully buried in the ground. Landfills cause pollution. As paper, food, and other wastes break down, large amounts of methane and carbon dioxide are released, contributing to global warming. Pollution from old landfills can slowly leak into the ground over time and affect the water we drink. Also, as old landfills become full, we are running out of space for new sites.

In many developing countries, people make a living by recovering valuable materials from garbage dumps. About 15 families live in houses made from recycled waste in the al-Taji garbage dump in Baghdad, Iraq. They sift through the waste for glass, plastic, or any other valuable material that they can sell.

In other countries, most garbage is burned in incinerators. That method of disposal takes less space than landfills and many people think it is safer. However, burning waste produces toxic ash, which needs to be buried. Some materials, such as plastics and textiles, release toxic gases in the air.

In many poor countries, millions of people living on the edge of expanding cities do not have any waste collection. They are forced to dump their garbage in streets, rivers, and ditches. However, in other ways poorer countries set a good example to wealthier nations. With limited resources, repair and reuse is often a common practice. Wood, metal, and plastic waste are often repurposed as building material for homes. Empty cans are turned into water containers. Old tires are made into sandals, and flammable materials are a source of fuel.

Nuclear Waste

To reduce our dependence on fossil fuels, many countries are opting for a different sources of energy, including nuclear power. Unlike fossil fuels, nuclear power produces very few emissions of polluting gases. However, it does produce highly toxic waste, which can take more than 20,000 years to become harmless. Nuclear waste is radioactive — it gives off invisible energy rays that can seriously harm people's health. Nuclear waste is currently buried in specially designed containers, but scientists are looking at better ways of getting rid of such dangerous waste. One possibility being explored by the United States is the long-term storage of high-level radioactive waste deep below Earth's surface. Many people are opposed to that option as no one can guarantee that waste will not leak.

WHAT WOULD YOU DO?

You Are in Charge

You are thrilled to get a new cell phone for your birthday. What do you do with your old cell phone?

- Give it to a family member or a charity.
- Send it back to the company that made it because they have a policy of recycling and reusing components.
- Send it to a company that reuses phone parts.
- Throw it out. It's so small it's not going to be a big problem in a landfill.

Think about a day in your life and all the things you buy, consume, and throw away. What three things could you do to help reduce the amount of waste you send to landfills or incinerators?

CHAPTER 5

A Different Way

It is 2025. Zara and her family have moved to their eco-home. The sides of the house use solar cells to capture energy from the sun. Grass grows on the roof to keep the house cool in summer and warm in winter. Gas produced from sewage is used for cooking. A small wind turbine fitted on the chimney generates electricity. Rainwater filtered by plants is collected for activities, such as washing clothes and watering the garden. The family bike or walk when they can and own a car powered by hydrogen. They turn food waste into compost for the garden, and repair and recycle as much as possible.

We Cannot Go on Like This

Earth is polluted because of the way we make and dispose of waste, power our vehicles, and use energy. Products are designed to have a short lifespan, so we produce mountains of garbage. We dig out natural resources to supply factories and power stations, leaving behind large amounts of toxic waste. We burn huge amounts of fossil fuels to produce energy, releasing toxic gases into the air. Those pollutants mix with rain, affecting rivers, lakes, and oceans. Untreated waste from factories and power stations is discharged into rivers and seas. Toxic waste is burned. Waste from the constant production of goods is buried in landfills all over the world. Some of the substances we produce

An activist from the environmental group Greenpeace, dressed as a polar bear, hugs a model of Earth at the opening ceremony of the 2007 United Nations Conference on Climate Change in Bali, Indonesia.

are so dangerous that they will have to be carefully monitored for thousands of years. That is not sustainable. We cannot carry on like this forever.

What Is Being Done?

Pollution ignores borders. A polluted river flows across countries, and global warming affects everyone in the world. As a global problem, pollution needs a global solution. In recent decades, some progress has been made. Political and business leaders have negotiated international agreements and passed laws to reduce pollution.

World leaders adopted the Montreal Protocol in 1987 to ban the production of chemicals damaging the ozone layer. In 1989, the Basel Convention regulated the movement of dangerous waste from one country to another. In 1992, 179 world leaders met to discuss environmental issues at an Earth Summit in Rio de Janeiro, Brazil. They produced a document called Agenda 21. It stressed the need to do more with fewer resources and to adopt cleaner technology. Agenda 21 promoted the idea that polluters are responsible for the waste they create and should pay to clean it up.

MAIN INTERNATIONAL AGREEMENTS ON POLLUTION

Date Adopted	Name of Agreement	Purpose
1972	London Dumping Convention	To regulate what can and cannot be dumped into the sea
1987	The Montreal Protocol	To protect the ozone layer by taking action to control global emissions of CFCs
1989	Basel Convention	To control the movement of hazardous waste from one country to another
1992	Climate Change Convention (Earth Summit)	To stabilize greenhouse gas emissions and encourage scientific research into climate change
1997	Kyoto Protocol	To tackle climate change and reduce carbon dioxide emissions

In 1997, an important agreement was adopted at an international conference in Kyoto, Japan, to decrease the amount of gases that industries produce. The Kyoto Protocol came into force in 2005. Two years later, further targets to reduce emissions were discussed at another summit in Bali, Indonesia.

Although those agreements have helped to reduce pollution, the problem is that many of them are voluntary. Governments that sign the agreements are not legally bound to enforce their standards. Even when those agreements become law, there are no penalties for governments that do not conform. Sometimes the biggest polluters do not join those agreements. For example, the United States is one of the world's largest emitters of carbon dioxide. However, as of 2009, it had not signed on to the Kyoto Protocol.

Learning From Nature

Some people believe that the best way to tackle pollution is to use technologies and systems that imitate the natural world. Nature uses resources efficiently. Everything is interconnected and materials are used and reused over and over again. Our current approach is to take natural resources from the earth and to transform them into materials that cannot be returned safely into the environment.

Some people are trying different ways of designing and making things to use resources more efficiently. Others are beginning to

TERMITE VENTILATION

Termite mounds were the inspiration for a new kind of ventilation system. Termites build their mounds in a certain way to maintain the temperature inside their nest despite varying conditions outside. Ventilation holes at the bottom of the mounds allow fresh air to enter. Hot, stale air is forced out of the top. Termites open and close those holes to adjust the temperature as needed. Buildings fitted with ventilation systems that mimic this natural system use up to 90 percent less energy for air conditioning than conventional buildings of the same size.

think of waste as a resource in its own right. Products that are no longer needed can be composted and turned into food for plants and animals. They could also be used as materials for new products.

Nature has many examples of materials and processes that we can copy. For example, we can design new buildings by looking at trees. The surface of the building can capture sunlight to produce energy through solar panels. Rain can be collected and filtered naturally by plants. It can then be used for activities that do not require pure water, such as flushing the toilet. We could even use a mechanism similar to a tree's roots to draw water from the ground.

In 2007, the Trott family built an eco-home in Normandy, France. Their house is made entirely from recycled and natural materials, such as old tires, aluminum cans, and glass bottles. They use renewable energy from the sun and wind, and harvest water from rain and snow. All waste is treated on site.

A better understanding of natural processes can allow us to maintain a comfortable lifestyle without damaging the planet. For example, nature was the model for a new kind of outdoor paint, developed in Germany, that resists dirt and mold. The paint's inventors were inspired by the white lotus flower, which always has immaculately clean leaves. The leaves are covered with microscopic needles. Dust or dirt falling on the leaves gets stuck on the needles. When a raindrop rolls across the needles, it picks up the dirt and carries it away. The paint uses a similar principle to keep itself clean, reducing the need for pollution-creating detergents.

In many countries, waste is a valuable resource. Here, toy vehicles made from recycled cans are on display at a market in Antananarivo, Madagascar.

Clean Production

Instead of spending time and money cleaning up pollution, why not use methods that do not pollute in the first place? Today, many governments and businesses are investing in cleaner technologies that will help conserve resources and reduce pollution. Those technologies include cars that run on electricity and producing electricity using solar energy. Engineers have also found a way to capture carbon produced by power stations, reducing gas emissions.

Thinking in cycles, as nature does, has led to many new developments. For example, leather sneakers can now be produced without any toxic products, so they can be composted at the end of their life. Books can be made of plastics and washable vegetable inks. When they are no longer needed, the inks can be washed off and they can be reprinted as different books. Think of all the trees that would save.

Other businesses are looking into leasing products to customers rather than selling them. Some are aiming to design products that can be taken apart and reassembled, so they never need to be thrown away. For example, a mobile phone could be leased to a customer for a number of years, then taken back when it is broken or needs upgrading. Instead of sending the old phone to a landfill, valuable parts could be taken out and reused in a new phone. The other parts could be recycled. As the famous physicist Albert Einstein said, if we want to solve problems, we need to think in a different way from the way we were thinking when we created the problem.

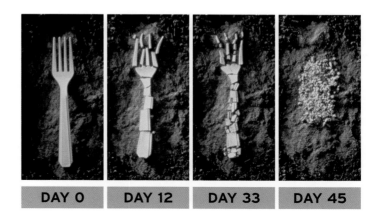

| DAY 0 | DAY 12 | DAY 33 | DAY 45 |

This fork, made out of a new kind of corn-based plastic, decomposes in just 45 days.

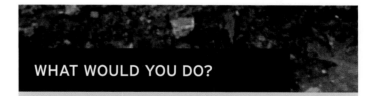

WHAT WOULD YOU DO?

You Are in Charge
You are an architect. A client has asked you to design a house of the future that mimics nature and reduces pollution.

- What materials would you use to build it?
- How would you design it in terms of its shape, size, and layout?
- What sources of energy would you use to provide its heat and electricity?
- How would you keep it cool in summer and warm in winter?
- What would you do to make sure the homeowner could minimize waste, and reuse and recycle as much as possible?

CHAPTER 6

Things You Can Do

It is 2025. More than half of the world's population is under 25 years old. Young people feel betrayed by the way their parents and previous generations have damaged the environment. They feel they are not being heard on issues that affect their lives. To give them a greater voice, an international youth summit on pollution is being held in Beijing, China. Working with the United Nations, that group of young people will represent their countries and help identify priorities for the next decade.

Personal Responsibility

Every time we use a computer, watch television, or cook a meal, we burn fossil fuels and pollute the atmosphere. Every time we throw out old clothes, CDs, or plastic bags, we add to the mountain of garbage produced each day. When we pour paint, oil, and other toxic substances down the drain or into rivers, we pollute the water we drink. By changing the way we consume goods, we can make a huge difference. Our own actions, combined with the actions of millions of others, can help reduce pollution.

Using Less Energy

A great deal of pollution is created by the energy we use to heat and light our homes, and power our vehicles. About 85 percent of the energy used in the world comes from burning fossil fuels, which releases carbon dioxide and other harmful gases. One way to reduce pollution is to use less energy at home, at school, and everywhere we go. If it gets cold, instead of turning up the heat, put on an extra sweater. The worst energy guzzlers in your house are clothes dryers, computers, and lighting. To save resources when using those items, switch off lights in empty rooms, turn off your computer when you are not using it, and unplug appliances with standby buttons.

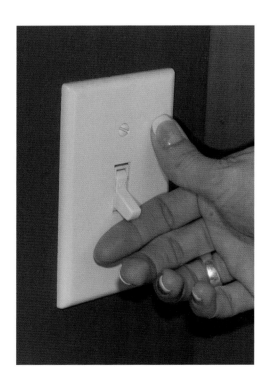

You can take action by using less energy at home. One way to reduce pollution is to switch off lights and tell the rest of your family to do the same.

Another way to save electricity is to use energy-efficient light bulbs. They use 75 percent less energy and last ten times longer than conventional bulbs. One downside to those bulbs is that they contain mercury, which can escape if the glass is broken. Make sure you dispose of old bulbs safely.

Also, why not use the sun to dry your clothes, power your calculator, or recharge your MP3 player? Talk to your family about the possibility of switching over to renewable energy, such as solar power. Another way you can save energy is by eating fruit and vegetables when they are in season. Growing strawberries in greenhouses in the winter, for example, uses a lot of electricity. Transporting fruit and vegetables from other countries also burns energy.

Solar power is an increasingly important energy source in many countries. Solar panels convert sunlight into electricity and can be used to provide heat and hot water for homes.

A LONG WAY TO THE DINNER TABLE

One study of a typical meal in the United States found that it used ingredients from at least five foreign countries. Those foods were imported, increasing pollution and carbon emissions levels worldwide. In 2005, fruit, vegetable, and nut imports to California alone caused more than 70,000 tons (63,503 tonnes) of carbon dioxide to be released, which is equivalent to 12,000 cars on the road for one year.

Source: www.farmlandinfo.org/documents/37291/foodmiles/pdf

Transportation accounts for about 13 percent of global greenhouse gas emissions. Walking or cycling does not create any pollution. It is good for your health and good for the environment. Flying less can also make a huge difference. Air travel is the fastest-growing form of transportation. It also produces about 3.5 percent of greenhouse gases. Why not cut down on flying and use trains whenever possible? Every mile traveled in a plane produces three times more carbon dioxide per person than traveling by train. Another way to reduce air travel is to buy locally-produced food. Buying local means less energy spent on transportation and packaging.

Buying Less, Wasting Less

If you buy less, then of course you throw away less. That saves natural resources and energy, and also reduces pollution. How many of the things you buy do you actually need or use regularly? You may want the latest game system, but is it really that much better than the old one? Will the old one end up in a landfill where it will take centuries to decay? Do you need to buy a brand new televison as soon as it hits the stores? Or could you wait a while and buy it used? Our personal choices influence the production of goods.

On average, each person in the United States throws out about 32 pounds (14.6 kilograms) of garbage each week. In the United Kingdom, the equivalent figure is 21.6 pounds (9.8 kilograms). The production of waste per person keeps growing. We are running out of space to bury our garbage and we pollute the atmosphere by burning it in incinerators. Although our personal garbage is a small part of the total waste produced on the planet, it is an important part.

We can change the way we buy, use, and dispose of products. For example, paper and cardboard fill about a fifth of our garbage cans. By using both sides of a piece of paper and buying fewer heavily packaged goods, we save trees, we reduce pollution, and we produce

Recycling helps to reduce pollution. For example, the energy needed to make one new aluminum can is the same as the energy needed to recycle 20 cans.

less waste. Reusing shopping bags also helps reduce the massive quantities of plastic bags littering the planet.

Reduce, Reuse, Recycle

The three Rs — reduce, reuse, and recycle — are good principles to follow to reduce pollution. In previous generations, people mended clothes, reused glass bottles, and even cleaned aluminum foil after use. Those were seen as valuable materials. We can adopt those same values today.

A woman displays a shopping bag made from old clothes. She was selling the bags at a creative bazaar promoting environmental awareness in Hubei Province, China, in 2008. Recycling can work only if we are prepared to buy products made from recycled materials.

Today, clothes are inexpensive and are often worn only for as long as they are fashionable. Yet the clothes we buy have a major impact on the environment. Toxic chemicals are sprayed on cotton crops and are used to dye fabrics. Fossil fuels are burned to power textile factories and transport those items around the world.

We can reduce the environmental impact of the clothing industry by thinking about the three Rs. Old clothes can be passed on to younger siblings, or given to charity for people who need them. They can also be recycled into new clothes, saving energy and reducing pollution. Recycling also reduces the need to harvest and mine new natural resources. Today, you can buy cotton T-shirts that can be composted, sweaters made from old plastic bottles, and belts made from old tires.

Students celebrate Earth Day in Los Angeles, California. Find out about Earth Day and plan a special event to raise awareness of the importance of reducing environmental pollution.

Protecting Water

We can help protect our water resources by thinking about what we pour down the drain or throw into rivers and streams. About 80 percent of the pollution in our oceans comes from the land. Many products we use in our homes contain toxic substances. Those include detergents, washing powders, shampoos, cosmetics, and oil-based paints. They can harm both our health and the environment. Yet there are often organic and all-natural alternatives that will do the same job without polluting our drinking water with harmful chemicals.

If we care about water quality, we should also avoid using pesticides and fertilizers in our gardens. Those toxic substances often end up in local water sources. Also, think carefully about how you dispose of garbage, or else your plastic bags and water bottles could end up adding to the Great Pacific Garbage Patch.

Speak Out

Talk to other people in your family, at school, or in the neighborhood about ways to reduce pollution. If enough people change their shopping habits, it could put pressure on your local supermarket to rethink where its food comes from, how it is packaged, and how it is transported. Why not write to your local newspaper about those issues? Find out about groups of concerned citizens hoping to make their voices heard in your local community, in your country, and in the world.

WHAT WOULD YOU DO?

You Are in Charge

You are doing the food shopping for the week and you want to help reduce pollution.

■ Where will you get your food from?

■ How will you get the food to your home?

■ What kind of cleaning products will you buy?

■ What kind of light bulbs will you buy?

■ What kind of fruit and vegetables will you buy?

■ What kind of red meat, chicken, or fish will you buy?

■ What kind of shopping bag will you use?

■ How will your weekly shopping change if you consider energy use, farming methods, transportation, packaging, and pollution?

PLEASE REUSE THIS BOOK

It takes about 17 trees to make one ton (.907 tonne) of paper, not to mention large amounts of water, and chemicals such as chlorine, sulfur, and energy. Please share this book with others so that many people read it.

Glossary

acid rain Rain that contains acid as a result of burning fossil fuels

atmosphere The layer of gases that surrounds and protects Earth. It is about 435 miles (700 kilometers) thick.

biodegradable Breaks down or rots naturally when attacked by bacteria such as food and garden waste

cadmium A metallic element found mainly in zinc, copper, and lead ores

carbon monoxide A poisonous gas produced when burning fuel, which mainly emitted from car exhausts

chlorofluorocarbons (CFCs) Chemicals used in products such as aerosols and refrigerators that deplete the ozone layer

compost A mixture of organic household waste that can be used as a fertilizer, such as vegetable peelings, brown cardboard, and plants that have decomposed over time

emissions Gases released into the atmosphere

fossil fuels Substances formed over a long period of time from the remains of dead plants and animals buried deep in Earth such as coal, oil, and natural gas

global warming The gradual increase in Earth's temperature, which most scientists believe has been caused by polluting greenhouse gases that have been trapping heat in the atmosphere

greenhouse effect The natural process by which heat is trapped in the atmosphere making life on Earth possible

greenhouse gases Gases, such as carbon dioxide and methane, that trap the Sun's heat and warm Earth. Scientists believe that increases in greenhouse gases are the result of man's activities and that those increases have led to global warming.

heavy metals Metallic elements that can be harmful to living things when they buildup in the food chain, such as chromium, mercury, cadmium, arsenic, and lead

herbicide A chemical designed to kill or weaken weeds

Industrial Revolution A rapid growth period of mass manufacturing that started in the late 1700s and was made possible by the invention of power-driven machinery, the development of the factory system, and the harnessing of energy from fossil fuels such as coal

nitrogen oxides Polluting gases formed from nitrogen and emitted when fossil fuels are burnt

oxygen A colorless, odorless gas found in abundance in the atmosphere that is vital for life

ozone A colorless, gaseous form of oxygen

ozone layer A layer of ozone high up in the atmosphere, which shields Earth from the Sun's harmful ultraviolet rays

particulate A substance that consists of separate particles, especially airborne pollution such as soot, dust, or fumes

pesticide A chemical designed to kill insects

photosynthesis The process by which plants convert sunlight, water, and carbon dioxide into food to release oxygen

plankton Microscopic marine organisms such as zooplankton, which are animals, and phytoplankton, which are plants

pollutant Something that contaminates air, soil, or water

power plant A facility where power, especially electricity, is generated

radiation Energy that is transmitted in the form of rays, waves, or particles

radioactive Describes elements, such as uranium, that emit radiation as they change into other elements

recycle To use materials that have been used before to make new things

smog A mix of smoke and fog that is produced by the reaction of hydrocarbons and nitrogen oxides in sunlight

solar energy Energy from the Sun that can be converted into heat or electricity

sulfur dioxide A polluting gas formed from sulfur that is emitted when burning fossil fuels

synthetic Describes substances and materials that are made by humans and do not occur in nature

toxic Poisonous to humans and other living things

ultraviolet rays A type of radiation made by the Sun that is harmful to plants, animals, and people

United Nations An organization of nations, formed in 1945 to promote peace, security, and international cooperation among its members

Further Information

Books

Boyer, Tristan. *You Can Save the Planet: Clean Planet: Stopping Litter and Pollution* (Heinemann, 2005)

Green, Jen. *Improving Our Environment: Air Pollution* (Wayland, 2007)

Jennings, Terry. *Save the Planet: Fight Air Pollution* (Chrysalis, 2005)

Leany, Cindy. *Your Environment: Pollution* (Franklin Watts, 2007)

Parker, Steve. *Green Files: Polluted Planet* (Heinemann, 2004)

Poddington, Lucy. *Understanding Pollution: Acid Rain* (Franklin Watts, 2006)

Web Sites

Global Cool
www.globalcool.org
Learn tips on how to use and lose less energy by changing your habits.

Greenpeace
www.greenpeace.org
Clean up the environment. The Greenpeace web site also includes tips for reducing global warming.

U.N. Environmental Programme
www.youthxchange.net
Read about pollution on this international web site to find out how the world's countries are reducing their impact on the environment.

U.S. Energy Information Administration
www.eia.doe.gov/kids
Learn more about pollution on the EIA's Kids page, a web site that offers facts about energy consumption, information about recycling, and activities and games.

U.S. Environmental Protection Agency
www.epa.gov/kids
Search the EPA's Environmental Kids Club, a web site for young people that provides facts about pollution and the environment and steps you can take to improve it.

Publisher's note to educators and parents:
Our editors have carefully reviewed these web sites to ensure that they are suitable for children. Many web sites change frequently, however, and we cannot guarentee that a site's future contents will continue to meet our high standards of quality and educational value. Be advised that children should be closely supervised whenever they access the Internet.

What Would You Do?

Page 11: Many people and organizations support the principle that polluters should pay. In other words, whoever causes pollution has to pay to clean it up. Businesses should pay for the disposal of the packaging and waste they create. Oil companies should pay for cleaning up spills. We, as consumers, should pay for the pollution and waste that we produce. If businesses and individuals know they will have to pay for the pollution they create, they are less likely to pollute in future. Nevertheless it is a good idea to pressure governments to set standards and guidelines so people know what actions they should take to minimize pollution.

Page 19: Today, most scientists agree that burning fossil fuel is responsible for global warming. However, there are different views about how we need to tackle that issue. Many people believe that the best plan for the future would be a combination of renewable energy and cleaner technologies. Nuclear energy does not generate air pollution but it produces toxic waste that can be dangerous for thousands of years. Finding ways to reduce our energy use is also a good idea.

Page 27: Oil spills can have a devastating effect on the environment. Oil companies are usually held responsible and asked to pay a fine. The company responsible for the *Exxon Valdez* oil spill was initially required to pay $5 billion. But in June 2008, that fine was reduced to a tenth of the original sum. Do fines really work? A key problem is that the fuels we use for energy are extracted in places far away from where the energy is eventually used. One solution is to look at ways of finding local energy sources, closer to where they are being used.

Page 33: The disposal of cell phones and other electronic items produces a huge amount of pollution because of the different materials and toxic components used to make those products. When recycling your cell phone, you need to make sure that you deal with responsible recyclers. To find out about recycling programs in your area, you can look at directories on the Internet.

Page 39: Mimicking nature means using nature as a model in the way we use natural resources and design things. In nature, everything is interconnected and materials are used and reused over and over again. When you design your house, ask yourself: "How does nature perform this function without creating any waste or pollution?" Try to use materials that can be composted or recycled. Try to avoid using toxic substances that pollute the environment and are often not necessary. Think about the natural water cycle and how to get water from the soil and from rainwater. Think about renewable sources of energy and how the shape of your house could help retain heat in cold weather or keep cool in hot weather.

Page 45: As a general rule, try to think about where your food comes from and how it has been produced. Did it have to travel thousands of miles to reach you or was it produced locally? Was it grown in season or produced in greenhouses, consuming lots of electricity? Was it produced with the use of chemical fertilizers and pesticides or grown organically? Check the labels to find out. Is the packaging necessary and, if so, is it made of materials that can be recycled or composted? One way of easily reducing pollution is to buy local produce from a farmers' market. Home delivery is also becoming more popular in many countries and helps to cut down on car dependence. And remember, you can make your voice heard by asking your local supermarket to stock more local organic produce.

Index

Page numbers in **bold** refer to illustrations and charts.

About the Author

Christiane Dorion has worked in education for sustainable development for more than 15 years with leading organizations, including the World Wildlife Fund and the Forum for the Future. She has written many educational books and specializes in global environmental issues.